The Rain Forest

Insects of the
Rain Forest

Mae Woods
ABDO Publishing Company

visit us at
www.abdopub.com

Published by Abdo Publishing Company 4940 Viking Drive, Edina, Minnesota 55435. Copyright © 1999 by Abdo Consulting Group, Inc. International copyrights reserved in all countries. No part of this book may be reproduced in any form without written permission from the publisher.

Printed in the United States.

Photo credits: Peter Arnold, Inc.

Edited by Lori Kinstad Pupeza
Contributing editor Morgan Hughes
Graphics by Linda O'Leary

Library of Congress Cataloging-in-Publication Data

Woods, Mae.
     Insects of the rain forest / Mae Woods.
     p. cm. -- (Rain forest)
     Includes index.
     Summary: Describes a variety of insects that live in the rain forest, and discusses some of their adaptations to that environment.
     ISBN 1-57765-023-9
     1. Rain forest insects--juvenile literature. [1. Rain forest insects.] I. Title. II. Series: Woods, Mae. Rain forest.
     QL467.2.W635   1999
     595.71734--dc21
                              98-11506
                                    CIP
                                    AC

Note to reader
The words in the text that are the color green refer to the words in the glossary.

Contents

Giant Insects.................................... 4

Stages of Life 6

Camouflage 8

Beetles 10

Flies 12

Ants 14

Termites 16

Bees 18

Butterflies 20

Glossary 22

Internet Sites 23

Index 24

Giant Insects

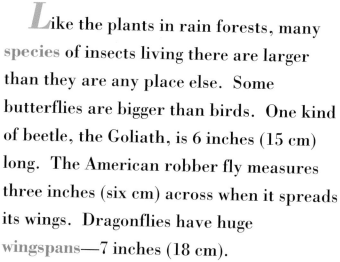

Like the plants in rain forests, many species of insects living there are larger than they are any place else. Some butterflies are bigger than birds. One kind of beetle, the Goliath, is 6 inches (15 cm) long. The American robber fly measures three inches (six cm) across when it spreads its wings. Dragonflies have huge wingspans—7 inches (18 cm).

There are five insect groups. Ants, bees, and wasps are one group of insects. Moths and butterflies are another. Three other groups are beetles, bugs, and flies. Many creatures, such as spiders, worms, and centipedes, are often called insects, but they are actually different species.

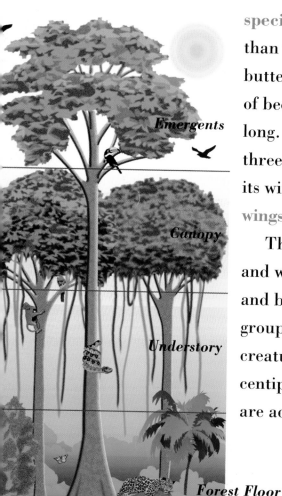

Emergents

Canopy

Understory

Forest Floor

Most rain forest insects live high up in the **canopy** levels among the trees and flowers. There they can make nests and find plenty of food. Some insects do not build nests. They make their homes in the fur of large animals. A **sloth** or gorilla may have many families of ticks, moths, and beetles living in its fur.

A leaf footed bug in a Malaysian rain forest.

Stages of Life

An insect's body can change during its lifetime. It is born in one form, called larva, and later becomes another. In the first part of a beetle's life, it is a soft, white grub. A fly starts life as a maggot. Butterflies and moths begin life as caterpillars.

A caterpillar is a puffy, tube-shaped larva that hatches from an egg. For about three weeks, the caterpillar feasts on leaves and grows. When the caterpillar has eaten enough, it turns into a fleshy pouch called a pupa. When this splits open, an adult butterfly will fly out. Most butterflies live two to four weeks.

Another way insects change their bodies is by molting, or shedding their skins. Insects have their skeletons outside of their bodies rather than inside. This hard, protective covering cannot stretch or

Pupa

expand. In order to grow, insects must break through their hard skins and develop new ones.

A Central American poisonous caterpillar.

Camouflage

*M*any insects in rain forests are difficult to see because they look like plants or other animals. This form of disguise is called camouflage. It allows them to hide from animals who would eat them. It also helps insects to sneak up on their prey. A katydid's wings look like the shape and color of a green leaf. The praying mantis's green color allows it to blend in with its surroundings. It waits among leaves looking for prey.

Some moths look like hummingbirds. Other moths look like leaves or tree bark. One special moth, called the io moth, has a pattern on its wings that looks like owl eyes. If a bird approaches, the io moth spreads its wings and quickly scares it away. The frightened bird thinks it is looking into the eyes of its enemy.

This katydid looks just like a leaf.

Beetles

Many of the insects that live on the floors of rain forests have special jobs to do. They eat all the dead leaves and branches that fall on the ground. Some types of insects eat dead animals. These materials pass through their bodies then go back into the soil as nutrients to feed new plants.

This "cleaning crew" includes beetles, ants, flies, termites, weevils, and cockroaches. There are so many of these insects that decaying things disappear very quickly. Dead leaves are on the ground for less than one day.

Beetles have hard protective coverings over their heads and bodies. Most beetles have delicate hind wings and can fly. Some, like ladybugs, are brightly colored. Most are black. One unusual flying beetle is the firefly. A firefly's body can glow. Their bright yellow lights allow males and females to find each other.

A beetle in the Amazon rain forest.

Flies

In its first stage of life, a fly is a maggot. This tiny white crawler looks like a worm. Maggots live in moist, rotting plants, dead animals, or in water. A maggot turns into a fly that has two wings and large, well-developed eyes. Their excellent vision makes them good hunters. Some species in the rain forests are fierce enough to attack bees and beetles.

Dragonflies live near water. They have unique life cycles. A dragonfly egg develops into a water insect called a naiad. When they reach adulthood, they crawl out of the water. A dragonfly will attach itself to a plant, shed its skin, then unfold its new wings and fly away.

Mosquitoes also begin life as water creatures. Mosquitoes feed on the blood of animals and people. It causes them to carry diseases from one person to another. In the tropics, people often sleep under fine nets to protect themselves from mosquito bites.

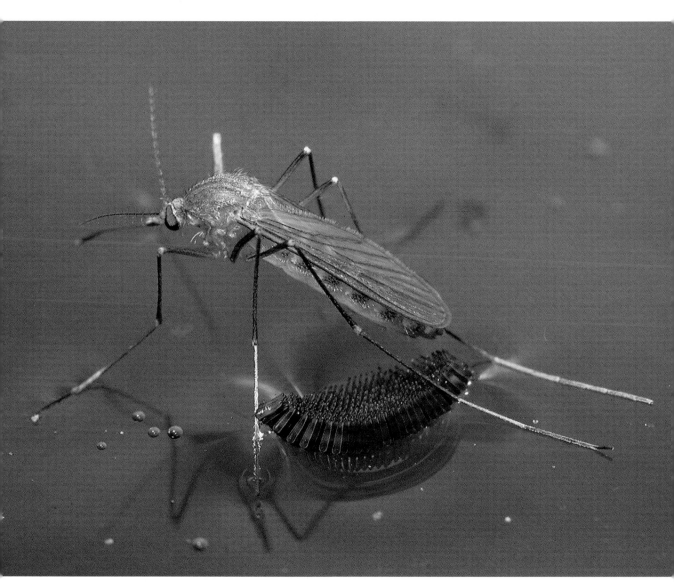

Mosquitoes begin life as water creatures.

Ants

There are more ants in rain forests than any other insect. Army ants live like military troops. They are always on the move. One colony may have twenty million ants in it. The small worker ants march in rows carrying food. Larger soldier ants protect the smaller ants from being attacked.

Weaver ants live in trees and bushes. They eat other insects. They bite their prey or spray them with poison. Baby ants, called grubs, make sticky threads that the weaver ants use to glue leaves together to make their nests.

Leaf-cutter ants live in underground colonies. Their large jaws work like scissors. A swarm of these ants can quickly nibble away an entire plant. They are unable to eat the leaves. They chew them into pulp and spit them out. An ant can eat the fungus that grows on the pulp. Making food keeps them busy. A colony needs seven pounds (three kg) of leaves a day to live.

Leaf-cutter ants working together.

Termites

*T*ermites live in underground colonies or in nests they build high up in trees. Each colony has one queen and king and many workers and soldiers. The queen makes thousands of eggs. Her huge abdomen may be 4 or 5 inches (10 or 13 cm) long. She lives in a chamber in the center of the nest. After she lays her eggs, the workers move them to a new room to hatch.

Termites eat wood. Some kinds of termites also eat leaves and seeds. The workers gather food for the whole colony and build the nest. There are many tunnels leading outside. Each entrance is protected by soldiers. The soldiers' jaws are so large that they cannot use them to eat. Workers must feed them. Most termites are blind. They have pairs of antennae on their heads that they use to feel their way around their nests.

Termites do not fight other colonies, but their nests are often attacked by ants and other animals. Frogs, lizards, birds, and anteaters like to eat termites.

A termite nest in a tree in Costa Rica.

Bees

Like ants and termites, a group of bees lives together in one large nest. A bee colony has one queen, lots of male bees called drones, and a large number of females who are the workers. Workers build nests, gather nectar and pollen, make honey, and guard their colonies.

The nest, called a hive, usually hangs inside a hollow branch. Together workers build a chain of wax cells into a comb. The queen lays eggs in these cells. There, each egg develops into larva and then pupa before the adult bee finally comes out. Combs are also used to store honey to feed the colony.

The queen bee and all the workers have stingers. The stinger is a hook attached to a gland. The gland makes poison. A bee uses its stinger to defend itself and its nest. The stinger can also be used to lay eggs.

A worker bee gathering pollen.

Butterflies

*B*utterflies love rain forests. Flowers bloom all year so there is always **nectar** to drink. The rain forest is a safe place, too. There are so many colorful plants that it is easy for butterflies to hide from animals who like to eat them. The urania butterfly has bright wings that blend in with flowers. Some butterflies have different markings under their wings to protect them. The underside of the red glider looks like a dull, brown leaf.

One of the most unusual butterflies is the morpho. It is bright blue with a 7 inch (18 cm) **wingspan**. Another huge butterfly, the giant swallowtail, grows to have a wingspan of 10 inches (25 cm). The birdwing butterfly has a wingspan of 8 inches (20 cm). It is very rare and lives high up in the trees.

Butterflies and moths are from the same group of insects. Butterflies fly during the day, and moths fly at night. Most moths are white. But in the rain forest some moths have beautiful, colored wings like butterflies.

A colorful butterfly
in Brazil.

Glossary

Abdomen - the lower part of an insect's body.

Canopy - the upper layer of the rain forest where most plants and flowers grow.

Chamber - a room.

Colony - a group of insects living together.

Disguise - things that are used to hide something or make it seem different.

Fungus - a growth formed during the process of decaying.

Gland - a part of the body that produces a fluid.

Grub - the larva of certain beetles and other insects.

Larva - the young worm-like form of an insect.

Maggot - the larva form of a fly.

Molting - shedding a skin or shell before getting a new covering.

Naiad - the young form of a dragonfly that lives in water.

Nectar - sweet liquid inside a flower.

Nutrients - (NOO-tree-ents) the food needed for the growth of plants or animals.

Pollen - a fine grain found inside a flower.

Prey - an animal that is caught to be eaten.

Pulp - a soft, wet mass.

Pupa - an insect in the stage of development between a larva and an adult.

Sloth - a furry animal that lives in trees and moves very slowly.

Species - a group of plants or animals that are alike in certain ways.

Wingspan - measurement across two wings that are spread open.

Internet Sites

Amazon Interactive
http://www.eduweb.com/amazon.html
Explore the geography of the Ecuadorian rain forest through on-line games and activities. Discover the ways in which the Quichua live off the land.

Living Edens: Manu, Peru's Hidden Rain Forest
http://www.pbs.org/edens/manu/
This site is about the animals and indigenous people who populate Peru's Manu region.

The Rain Forest Workshop
http://kids.osd.wednet.edu/Marshall/rainforest_home_page.html
The Rain Forest Workshop was developed by Virginia Reid and the students at Thurgood Marshall Middle School, in Olympia, Washington. This site is one of the best school sites around with links to many other sites as well as great information on the rain forest.

The Tropical Rain Forest in Suriname
http://www.euronet.nl/users/mbleeker/suriname/suri-eng.html
A multimedia tour through the rain forest in Suriname (SA). Read about plants, animals, Indians, and Maroons. This site is very organized and full of information.

These sites are subject to change. Go to your favorite search engine and type in Rain Forest for more sites.

Pass It On

Rain Forest Enthusiasts: educate readers around the country by passing on information you've learned about rain forests. Share your little-known facts and interesting stories. Tell others about animals, insects, or people of the rain forest. We want to hear from you!

To get posted on the ABDO Publishing Company website E-mail us at **"Science@abdopub.com"**

Visit the ABDO Publishing Company website at www.abdopub.com

Index

A

animals 5, 8, 10, 12, 16, 20
ants 4, 14, 18

B

bees 4, 12, 18
beetles 4, 10, 12
birds 4, 8, 16
butterflies 4, 6, 20

C

canopy level 5
caterpillars 6
colony 14, 16, 18

D

disease 12
dragonflies 4, 12
drones 18

E

eggs 6, 16, 18

F

firefly 10
flowers 5, 20
food 5, 14, 16

G

gland 18
grub 6, 14

L

ladybugs 10
larva 6, 18
life cycle 12

M

maggots 6, 12
molting 6
mosquitoes 12

N

naiad 12
nectar 18, 20
nests 5, 14, 16, 18

P

plants 4, 8, 10, 12, 20
pollen 18
praying mantis 8
prey 8, 14
pulp 14
pupa 6, 18

S

species 4, 12
spiders 4

T

termites 10, 16, 18
trees 5, 14, 16, 20
tropics 12

W

wings 4, 8, 10, 12, 20